LEARN.
UNLEARN.
RELEARN.

How to live the life you desire
through the transformation of your beliefs
and behaviours

Tafadzwa Makombe, CA (SA)

REVIEWS

"This book came at a perfect stage of my life. I recently changed jobs and shortly after the national COVID lockdown started. It gave me a better perspective on how to view and tackle obstacles that came with the new role. It assisted me in dealing with the imposter syndrome experienced in the first few months and I really appreciate the timing of it. Much appreciated Tafadzwa."

—Snegugu Vilakazi CA (SA)

"This book takes a seeker on a journey to self-discovery not only by providing helpful tools, but by also taking the reader's hand and walking them step-by-step through the power of the mind. It helped me realize how mastering the power of your subconscious mind can transform your life. If you believe that your greatest breakthrough in life is only delayed but not denied, grab a copy of this book and the benefits will be worth it."

—Rhulani Hlongwane (Entrepreneur)

"'Remember that you are the ARCHITECT OF YOUR LIFE!' Powerful words we all hear but are mostly guilty of never applying. Tafadzwa's book, **_Learn. Unlearn. Relearn._**, not only breaks down the accountability and responsibility that you have as the architect of your life but she also shows you pragmatically how to design your blueprint and manifest it into reality. If you are looking to take full accountability and responsibility for who you really are, then this is the book for you."

—Grant Senzani
Author, Speaker, and Serial Entrepreneur

"The book is an essential for everyone's bookshelf and is full of practical advice and exercises to help you live your ideal life. A definite must-read for those who are serious about transforming their lives."

—Ntombizodwa Tshongwe

TABLE OF CONTENTS

FOREWORD

This book gives the reader insight into and the confidence to face their experiences in learning that the mind is a fascinating tool to learn, unlearn, and relearn themselves. It also teaches the reader how to venture into a new territory of self-actualization. Knowing how to be effective and mastering the power of your subconscious mind allows you to get rid of the negative emotions and gain knowledge of how to conquer yourself and the world.

The author provides incredible tools for one to be able to do their introspection through the questions that she has provided. These questions offer an opportunity for the reader to understand what beliefs are; the limiting beliefs they currently hold in their life; and who planted those limiting beliefs as they grew and developed. Understanding our limiting beliefs is important so that we can identify the negative self-talk and turn those negative conversations to positive ones. It gives us a way to be able to be more effective in our personal life and the environment around us. When you gain the ability to get your subconscious mind to serve you to its full potential you are then able to set more achievable goals.

A great thank you to the author who is my friend and colleague for writing this book to share her knowledge on what can make us more than awesome human beings.

I would like to acknowledge her courage in stepping out of her comfort zone and using her life experiences to help others.

With Love,

Miss Zama Khanyile
—*Social Worker, EAP Therapist, and Qualified Transformational Life Coach*

DEDICATION

This book is dedicated to every person who finds themself already in their grave, that longed to transform their life but never knew how.

ACKNOWLEDGMENTS

I would like to thank Grant Senzani from
The Golden Goose Institute (Pty) Ltd and Sonia Dube from
Renascense for guiding me through the process of
writing my first book and assisting me in the successful
self-publishing of this book.

Thank you to Motsanephe Morare from
MoMa-LifeLiving for creating the illustrations for this book
(except where otherwise referenced).

Thank you to my friend, Didintle Letlape,
for seeing my potential in 2017 and
pushing me to stop remaining a prisoner to my negative
past experiences and limiting beliefs.
Thank you for encouraging me to self-develop which
resulted in me realizing my full potential.

INTRODUCTION

Human beings are made up of 3 parts; these being the mind, body, and spirit (also known as the soul). People would typically subscribe to either religion or spirituality to master their spirit and tap into the infinite power of their Creator, or a Higher Power, to find purpose in their life and receive inspiration and wisdom to conquer life's challenges. To obtain mastery over their body, a person would normally look towards a personal trainer for home or gym workouts, or would get a sports coach to help them train for a marathon or sports match so they can win and be the best. Most people have forgotten that their <u>mind</u> also requires a coach or trainer so that they can cultivate the best mindset to apply in their life to become the best version of themselves; obtain their desires; and achieve their goals. Remember that you are made up of three parts and for you to perform at your optimum and live the happiest and best possible life you can live, you need to ensure that <u>all</u> three parts are functioning at their peak.

This is why I have chosen to write this book. As a life coach, I coach and guide my clients to master their minds so they can transform their life to obtain the desires they seek. As a result, they can master their lives in all areas, whether it is wealth, career, depression, anxiety, public speaking, relationships, physical appearance or spiritual well-being. In the same way that all top athletes have coaches that train them to become the best, I will coach you to ensure you live your best life!

I titled this book **Learn. Unlearn. Relearn.** because that is the key to transforming your life. By the time you are an adult, you would have had at least 21 years of conditioning starting from the moment you were conceived - based on your genetics and upbringing - which results in the behaviours you currently action out every day. This conditioning is influenced by your beliefs, culture, religion, language, race, memories, values, and meta-programming. In other words, you behave in a certain way and hold a certain view of life because of all those factors that conditioned your thinking and behaviours. This means that no one sees the world the exact same way that you do; we all have our own unique map of the world.

Our conditioning either empowers our behaviour or it restricts us due to limiting beliefs that we have been taught by those around us or that were developed through negative experiences. This process was the *"Learn."* phase where you discovered all your beliefs about what is true about the world and what is possible for you to achieve. In order to transform your life and obtain your desires, you need to unlearn all the negative and limiting beliefs you were brought up with and relearn new positive and empowering beliefs so that you can start behaving in a more empowered way. Reading this book will guide you through the *"Unlearn."*

and "*Relearn.*" processes of your transformation, and many of my clients will testify to the incredible results they manifest within a few days of completing them.

People are not looking for you, they are looking for what you are carrying inside of you. And if you do not manifest what you are carrying, the world will ignore you. Just because you exist doesn't mean you are going to be successful in life. You can live on earth but that doesn't mean people will notice you. You can live an entire lifetime to the age of 90 years old and still not be noticed by humanity. We can bury you in a cemetery and no one will know you ever existed except for that tombstone. Most people live on earth but never fulfill the manifestation of the best version of themselves; therefore, your most important goal in life should be self-manifestation.

Please do not be hard on yourself if the concepts I discuss in this book do not click the first time around. I also didn't understand them at first, especially the information relating to the subconscious mind! Go over them as many times as you need to until you fully understand the principles because once you do, only then can you effectively apply them and transform your life. I know you will thoroughly enjoy the transformation process though. Please don't forget to share your experiences and eye-openers with me once you are done with this book. Feel free to email me at taffy@elevatetransformationcoaching.com. I genuinely look forward to hearing your success stories of how you turned your life around.

Chapter 1:

MIND POWER

"Whatever we plant in our subconscious mind and nourish with repetition and emotion will one day become a reality."

—Earl Nightingale

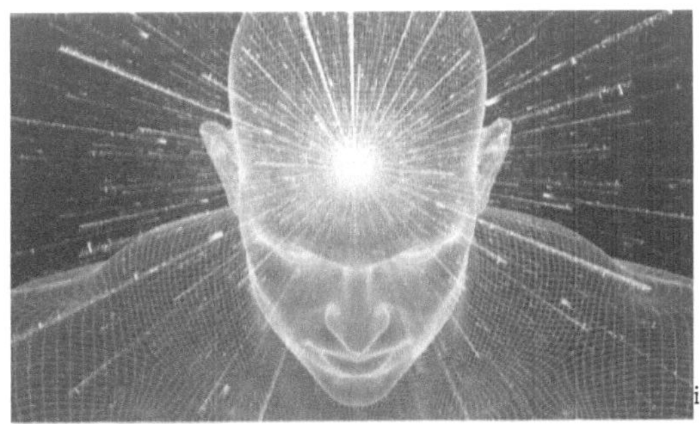

I am about to share information on our powerful brains. Information that I wish I had known earlier in life because then I would have been so much further by now.

Scientists have proven that we have several neurons in every cell in our body and not just in our brain as previously thought. Deepak Chopra in his book, **Quantum Healing**, published in 1986, proved that neurons are everywhere in the body and that as we learn new things, we grow new neurons. Each neuron has the potential of $(1010)^{11}$ neurological connections. That is the number 10 with ten zeros behind it, written eleven times! You literally have more possible neurological connections than the total number of stars in our visible universe or all the grains of sand on all the beaches on our planet. This means that your brain can communicate with any part of your body instantly. Your thoughts are being communicated to all of your cells all of the time. This proves that there is a mind-body connection. Your thoughts about yourself and your body have a direct impact on your health, physical state, and mental well-being. For instance, when you feel stressed or sad have you noticed that your body becomes lethargic and lazy and your posture becomes crouched? Whereas if you are happy or in love your posture is upright, you have a bounce in your step, and your chin is held up high. The mind-body connection means that your thoughts have a direct effect on every single cell in your body. With the correct mindset, beliefs, and emotional state we can reshape our bodies and improve our health.

We are not hard-wired; our brain and intellect are plastic. Previously, until as recently as only 1990, scientists believed our brain was hard-wired and could not be re-programmed. However, your body has the incredible power of rewiring itself but this of course is only possible if you choose to do something about it. It can change, create new neural pathways, make new connections, and retract old ones. The problem is that a lot of doctors, physiologists, psychiatrists, and teachers are still working on the old and outdated model of the brain. Therefore, most of them are still limiting us in a big way. That is why they think they need to give us drugs to "fix" us instead of finding the root cause and then resolving it.

Our brain is made up of the conscious mind and sub-conscious mind. The conscious making up 5% of the brain and the subconscious making up the remaining 95%. Your subconscious mind stores all your memories, emotions, beliefs, habits, behaviours, values, programming, and instincts. Change occurs in the **subconscious mind** which means that you can change everything about yourself and your results in life by changing the current blueprint embedded in your subconscious mind. But before we get there you need to learn more about the subconscious mind and what it specifically does.

This is how I want you to imagine the immense power and size of your subconscious mind: I will use an illustration of an iceberg. Normally, when we see icebergs on TV we are only shown the tip of the iceberg found on the surface of the water. What we don't see is that beneath the surface of the water there is a huge mass of ice which is ten times bigger than the ice above the surface. The ice above the surface of the water represents your conscious mind while the ice below it signifies your subconscious mind. Think about that for a while. Your power to transform your life lies in your subconscious mind! This also illustrates how we are limited in terms of seeing the bigger picture. We are conditioned to settle for what we can see.

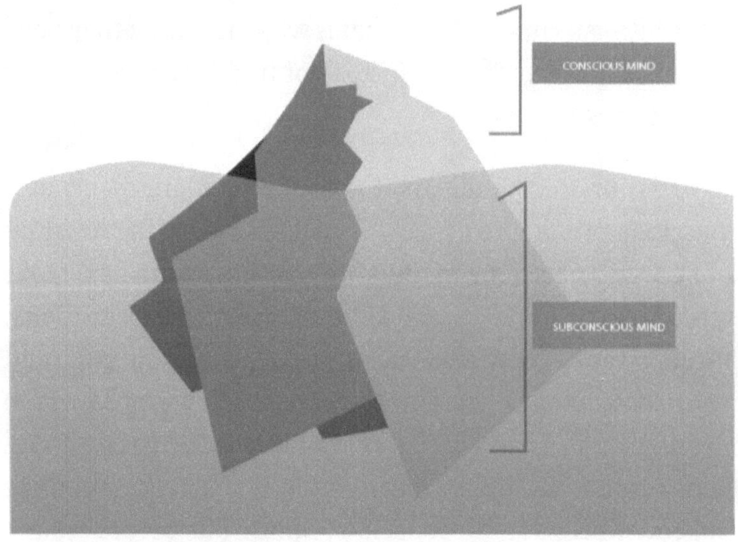

As a result of the mind-body connection, your subconscious mind is stored in all the neurons in your body and every cell in your body is thus affected by the thoughts and emotions that are in your subconscious mind. When you have a lot of unprocessed, unresolved negative emotions such as anger, frustration, sadness, fear, hurt, doubt, hate, shame, anxiety, and guilt they will have a negative impact on your whole body and not just your mind. That can cause a lot of unwanted behaviours, symptoms, and diseases.

Here are a few characteristics of the **subconscious mind**:

- It controls 97% of your perceptions and behaviours.
- It is like your computer's operating system. It is technically your Windows running in the background controlling your breathing, heart rate, and the running of your body, etc.
- It is the domain of your emotions.
- It stores all your memories.
- It represses memories with unresolved negative emotions to protect you because continuously facing your baggage will drive you crazy. The subconscious mind uses a lot of energy to suppress these negative emotions so by releasing them most people experience much more energy in their day-to-day living.
- It presents repressed memories for resolution.
- It averages 10 billion-plus actions/calculations per second!
- It controls and maintains all perceptions received through the five senses and transmits the information to the conscious mind.

- It generates, stores, distributes, and transmits energy.
- It maintains instincts and generates habits.
- It is programmed to seek more and more; everything in nature is designed for expansion and growth and the subconscious mind is no different.
- It operates in pictures, symbols, and patterns.
- It does not know the difference between the truth or a lie. It gives you what you focus on. It accepts everything as truth. It cannot tell real from imagined; it believes everything to be the absolute truth, whatever you send it – be it an image, picture, or sound.
- It enjoys serving you by creating more of what you dominantly focus on and give attention to; however, it needs clear orders of what it is that you choose to have. It will attract the right people and circumstances into your life to help you reach your outcomes and goals if you let it.
- It does not process negatives. Meaning that if you tell someone not to do something, they will do it. For example, if you tell your kids: "Do not jump on the bed", the "not" cannot be processed by the subconscious mind. All they hear is "Do jump on the bed". Instead of telling someone what not to do, rather tell them exactly what they should do or exactly how to behave. Using this example, rather tell your kids, "We sleep on the bed and we jump on the trampoline outside." This works for adults as well as children.

Your conscious mind, on the other hand, is responsible for thinking and reasoning. The conscious mind can accept or reject any idea, unlike the subconscious mind that accepts everything as true. The conscious mind is the guard to the great and powerful subconscious mind. Here are a few characteristics of the **conscious mind**:

- Controls 3% of your perceptions and behaviours.
- It is supposed to be the Captain of the subconscious mind which is the true change-maker for every individual. The thoughts you consistently choose and impress on your subconscious from your conscious mind will determine the results in your life.
- It is the guardian/guard to the subconscious mind. Its job is to allow only positive life-giving information through to the subconscious mind.
- This is where your will power and reasoning reside.
- It is time-bound, meaning it mainly focuses on the past and the future.
- It has limited processing capacity – approximately 2 000 bits of information per second.
- It can only focus on 1 – 3 things at a time.

The Reticular Activation System

Your Reticular Activation System (RAS) is the filtering system that screens information coming in through all five of your senses before it goes to your conscious mind. Your five senses being:

- Sight – Visual (V)
- Hearing – Auditory (A)
- Feeling – Kinesthetic (K)
- Smell – Olfactory (O)
- Taste – Gustatory (G)

Your senses receive approximately 400 billion bits of information per second from the world and that information passes through your RAS and gets deleted, distorted, and generalized, which as a result reduces the information you truly absorb into your mind to about 2 000 bits of information per second. The RAS forms part of your subconscious mind and functions up to 800 times faster than your conscious mind. Literally, every sensory impulse received will go through it first. There, the RAS decides whether the information received is important to you or not. In other words, it will pass the information received to your conscious mind ONLY if the information received is on your priority list. For example, if the impulse received is the sound of an alarm siren, your RAS will quickly prioritize it for you, passing this information to your conscious mind and grabbing your attention regardless of what you were busy with at the time. This happens because the alarm sound is on your priority list with your mind being conditioned to act upon hearing a siren.

This means that you need to upload into your RAS only what is important to you. This is exactly why when you focus so much of your attention on problems such as debt, all your RAS can bring to your attention is more of what you have stressed as important. If you constantly worry about debt, debt will impress itself on your priority list, and your RAS will do whatever it can to bring more of it to your attention. Just think about this. We genuinely create and attract more fear, worries, depression, illness, unhappiness, and anger when we focus on that constantly.

Remember, its job is to find, in the outside world, everything that matches your inside world. For this reason, we need to control our inside world first, so that we can see it in our physical, outside world. This is how we constantly create and recreate ourselves and our realities. We are, today, the result of past thinking and what we are thinking today we shall be in the future. The RAS seeks information that validates your beliefs. It filters the world through the parameters you give it, and your beliefs shape those parameters. If you think you are bad at giving speeches, you probably will be. If you believe that you work efficiently, you most likely do. The RAS helps you see what you want to see and in doing so, influences your actions.

You can train your RAS by taking your subconscious thoughts and marrying them to your conscious thoughts. They call it "setting your intent." This basically means that if you focus hard on your goals, your RAS will reveal the people, information, and opportunities that will help you achieve them. If you care about positivity, for example, you will become more aware of and seek positivity. If you really want a pet turtle and set your intent on getting one, you'll tune in to the right information that helps you do that. Owning a pet turtle will manifest in your life as a result of you tuning in to the different pet stores available to get one or what sort of tank or habitat to buy for it, and the kind of food required so that you are prepared once you get the turtle. When you look at it this way, the Law of Attraction doesn't seem so mystical. Focus on the bad things and you will invite negativity into your life. Focus on the good things and they will come to you because your brain is seeking them out. It's not magic, it's your Reticular Activating System influencing the world you see around you.

The Amygdala

The amygdala is an almond-shaped brain structure involved in memory and emotional processing. It has tremendous power over your perception and actions. It senses potential or real stress and then orders the release of stress hormones. This causes you to have doubts, fear, or anxiety. The amygdala deals with your emotions, helps process memories, and gets absorbed in managing your response to fear and stress. From birth, we all have a built-in automatic response system that triggers a fight or flight reaction to what you perceive as an "emergency event". The amygdala's job is to determine how to respond to a "wow" type of event, be it an emergency, something that simply startles you, or any type of event that produces an emotional response. In so responding, the amygdala causes the release of neuro-hormones such as adrenaline and cortisol into the body which causes the "fight or flight" reaction.

In addition to interpreting incoming sensory information, the amygdala is involved in processing memory, particularly memories with emotional impact. Given how intense emotions can be, perhaps you can understand why memories tagged with emotions would be among the strongest memories we have. However, if you get stressed over something, the stress response may make it more difficult for you to recall a specific memory. It will inhibit your ability to think clearly.

What does this information have to do with me achieving my goals? Well, most of us tend to respond to the amygdala signal by simply stepping back into our comfort zone. There is a great benefit to learning to manage, assess, and take control of the fight or flight response generated by the amygdala. It would be beneficial if we were able to respond to the amygdala response with clarifying questions before taking action. If you are going to create the life you want or achieve your goals, you have to be able to step out of your comfort zone and stay out.

Please understand that these systems are all a part of you, designed to serve and protect you. You should learn as much as you can about them and programme them to serve your current thinking and goals, instead of having no choice but to react in the way that you always have and thus not moving forward in your life.

The Psycho-Cybernetic Mechanism

The psycho-cybernetic mechanism is in charge of keeping you in your comfort zone. It does not matter how bad your current situation is or how badly you want it to change; when it picks up any deviation from your comfort zone, it sends feedback to your nervous system. Your nervous system then tries to "correct" the deviation by creating an emotional stimulus to your amygdala to bring you back to your comfort zone.

For example, a salesperson who works on a commission-based salary may decide to earn double what he did the previous month. Logically, this will require longer working hours, twice as many calls, and probably some other sacrifices. In return, after a week or so, his income would be higher in comparison to the previous month's income. At this point, his psycho-cybernetic mechanism would kick in and send neural transmitters to cause doubts, fear, and anxiety. It will cause him to rationalize things. Please bear in mind that this happens automatically and so fast that you have no idea it is happening at all. It will start justifying old behaviours. This salesperson might find it perfectly reasonable to take a break since he has worked so hard. The psycho-cybernetic mechanism will literally find a dozen excuses for why you should relax a bit and slow down. All this is to bring you back into your old comfort zone. What's important to note is that it does not know if you are happy or unhappy in your comfort zone; its job is simply to keep bringing you back there. This is a critical point to take note of. Without resetting this system, nothing will change! This system causes you to consistently behave that way; continuously bringing you back to your old state and behaviours.

The opposite of familiarity is the unknown. When you were a child, almost everything was unknown. Each day brought new exploration and a new set of possibilities. When you learnt to walk you kept going even if you fell, getting back up each time, over and over, always smiling. You kept doing this because of your unshakeable desire and belief that you would walk. You will find people with lives that they did not dream of; they might be in dead-end jobs that barely pay the bills for instance. However, at least they have the comfort of knowing what tomorrow will look like, no matter how depressing or boring it may seem. They know that although it is not the life of their dreams - in fact, it is probably more of a nightmare - they are used to this life. Their need for certainty is so strong and overwhelming that they end up settling for less, staying where they are, and not allowing themselves to experience the unknown.

To change your psycho-cybernetic mechanism, you need to continually bridge your comfort zone. It will always feel uncomfortable in the beginning and this is where you have to use your willpower and keep pushing forward. Within a short period, you will get comfortable again. This is when it is time to bridge your comfort zone again and start moving onto the next level. The more you do it, the easier it becomes and the faster you start growing to achieve success in life.

Chapter 2

BELIEFS CREATE YOUR REALITY

"Many people are passionate, but because of their limiting beliefs about who they are and what they can do, they never take actions that could make their dream a reality."

—Tony Robbins.

Our thoughts are real! Your thought is not just a thought; it is a material thing made up of energy. In fact, thoughts are the most potent energy known to us! To date, they are the highest form of vibrating energy that scientists have ever measured. Think about that carefully. Our thoughts create! Look at your table or your cellphone or any man-made object. How did they become a physical man-made object? All these objects started as a thought. So what are you creating with your thoughts?

Everything that you are currently experiencing in your outside world is a mere reflection of what is happening in your inside world. If there is chaos and havoc in your outside world that means that there is chaos and havoc in your inside world. The inside world reflects directly onto the outside world. Take a moment to ponder that... Are you still reading? No! Seriously think about it for a minute. How is your outside world now? Now look deeply inside yourself and have a good look at your inside world. Can you see how your inside world reflects onto your outside world? If you have conflict, struggle, hate, anger, depression, and low self-esteem within, it will return to you from the outside world.

The way to get in control of your outside world is definitely not to try and control the outside world. I am sure you have tried that before and found that it does not work. We do not have the power to control the people and circumstances in the outside world. The best way to get lasting results in the outside world is to start getting control of your inside world where **you** have the **power**.

Most of it you created unconsciously. Meaning you were not aware consciously that you were creating or causing it. Stop trying to constantly change your outside world, but instead: change yourself from the inside. STOP expecting your mirror to smile first at you. You need to learn to smile first before your mirror reflects that back at you.

What is a Belief, Really?

Beliefs are ideas and concepts you accepted either unconsciously or consciously. They run like programmes on autopilot in the subconscious which operate like background programmes on computers (think of the example of a software programme running on a computer). These programmes/beliefs create your reality. You are 50% predisposed to your behaviours. Everything else, you learnt through experience. Your beliefs process only energy and emotions to create your reality.

Positive beliefs, without any effort from your side, automatically create a positive reality. The problem is that negative beliefs, without you knowing it and without any effort, automatically create a negative reality for you on autopilot. All negative or limiting beliefs are attached to negative or unwanted feelings: they are in a marriage with each other. The more we let go of negative beliefs during the day, the more we are letting go of masses of negative thought patterns. Just by letting go of 1 negative belief that got triggered during the day, you are letting go of 1000 negative thought patterns that normally get triggered by that one negative belief. By continuously letting go of all unwanted beliefs as they come up during the day, we are quietening the mind and slowly eliminating the EGO.

You have to ask yourself: what caused the results in my life? This is regardless of whether or not they are the ones you actually want! They are linked to your actions and past behaviours based on the decisions you have made in your life. You attract and therefore create everything in your life. Genetically, you are 50% predisposed to your behaviours. Everything else you had to learn through experience. Your parents, friends, school teachers, etc. have influenced you. Through your interactions with them, you have formed what you believe today to be the truth. However, we have learnt that what we know is not the complete truth – it is only our perception of the truth. For you, the truth is what you strongly believe in, and that is only because you have beliefs in your mind confirming that. Firm beliefs are created simply by experiencing something repeatedly over a period. It then becomes the truth for us.

(Seeing + Listening + Doing + Experiencing) x Repetition
= Beliefs
What are habits?
Behaviours x Repetition = Habits

Your behaviours, internal and external, are derived from your beliefs. If you repeat a behaviour numerous times over an extended period, it will become a habit. Habits, due to their practical nature, have a significant impact on our results. Habits are behaviours that run on autopilot, regardless of how beneficial the results are that they produce.

Perception is Projection

As I mentioned in Chapter 1, we can now measure up to 400 billion bits per second being received via our 5 senses from the world and only about 2 000 bits per second being processed by our conscious mind. Massive amounts of information get dropped and never reach our conscious mind. I am repeating what I stated earlier allowing you to link information supplied with what you already know. Remember that 400 billion bits per second gets filtered down to only 2 000 bits per second and presented to our conscious mind as the reality that we live in. This would mean that based on our wiring, our filters, our model of the world, maps, etc. we get to perceive the world in our unique and individual way. Your 2 000 bits of information will not be the same as mine. Everyone filters the information differently. We delete, distort, and generalize information in our own way based on our filters. My filters are not the same as yours. Therefore, no two people will get the same information. Each will be based on that person's unique filtering system (RAS).

The world is not what it seems to be; you perceive just one small version of it. People cannot be in our lives any other way than what we project them to be. We cannot perceive anything from the outside world that is not already wired inside. Also, you cannot perceive the people around you for who they really are. You can only perceive one version of them - the one that has to do with you. Our filters are not the same - we only experience what is left of the information. That means that you cannot perceive anything from the outside world that is not in you. Perhaps a heavy statement but it is true. Your subconscious mind will project these things for you; it will get you to perceive things in a way that is aligned with your current wiring. You will experience things that you need to experience, and learn the learnings needed for you to grow and expand.

This is the basis of "Perception is Projection". The event is never something good or bad. Until we process the information and place our judgment on it based on our internal values, our belief systems, and our subconscious mind, we will get to experience the event only in a certain way and not in the way it really is.

Let us say, in a room of five people, somebody brings each of them a huge portion of some delicious cake. I guarantee that each of these people will experience this very same event, very same gesture, in their own unique way. Some will be insulted since they did not order any cake, and some will simply eat that cake with a huge smile on their face. Some, perhaps not satisfied with their weight, might have angry thoughts towards this person who brought the cake. They might even curse the cake bringer for just wanting them to get fatter. Lastly, some will appreciate the nice and thoughtful gesture. I am sure you can see where this is going and how our perception greatly alters the events that surround us, so much so that we all get to experience life differently. This is how we project what's inside of us to the outside world which is why I often say: "May you find what you seek outside, inside of you".

In life, we always act like the person we believe we are. That decision of choosing who and what we are is solely ours! Do you wear those so-called "jackets" of depression – some kind of illness, unworthiness, sin, not-good-enough attitude, guilt, hurt, or even anger? If that is what you see and believe, then you are right.

Why do you allow yourself to become hostage to the negative influences in your life? Whoever it is that told you that you *could not* showed no belief in you. They told you that you are worthless, unacceptable, or that others are brighter and more talented than you. Well, that can be correct if you, and only you, allow it to be. The decision is yours and yours alone. Something can only hurt if you choose for it to hurt. Put what they said in the past because that is what it is - the past. You know more now than you did then and because of that fact you have more going for you today than you did before. You can use all that past learning to empower yourself and have a more fulfilled and happier life than you ever imagined possible. So why do we choose to use our past as our excuse for pain, illness, depression, negativity, anger, hurt, and discomfort? It is over. Let go and move on. USE your learnings and let go!

What benefit do we get by advertising our flaws to others and ourselves? Too often we eagerly discuss our flaws and failures with people who are willing to listen. We pass out invitations to a masked pity party and unmask our disbelief in ourselves. Decide what you want to be, make goals to get there, and then create action steps to reach that destination. Most people live in the world without; few have found the world within. Yet the world within generates the world without. The world within is creative and everything you find in your world without you have created from your world within. The world within is the cause and the world without is the effect. To change the effect, you must change the cause. Stop allowing the world without to control your world within.

Exercise:

1. Ask yourself: what limiting beliefs have I been raised to believe are true that are holding me back from living the life that I want?

    ____

    ____

    ____

2. Write down the experience/person/people that taught
    you this limiting belief:

    ____

    ____

    ____

3. Write down why these limiting beliefs are NOT true:

    ____

    ____

    ____

Chapter 3

EMOTIONS FUEL YOUR ACTIONS

*"Negative emotions are like unwelcome guests.
Just because they show up on our doorstep
doesn't mean they have a right to stay."*

—Deepak Chopra

Now, let's talk about emotions. I mentioned before that your subconscious mind is also the emotional part of you. Emotions play a huge role in conditioning your mind. Whenever you experience something very powerful and emotional your brain will react with and release chemicals and proteins, while simultaneously sending information down the newly created neuro-pathways, growing the instantaneous highways per se. This is how we can create strong, dominant beliefs in an instant. This process can happen in an instant and the perfect example is phobias. When we experience a great fear or near-death experience, new beliefs are created instantaneously. For example, it may be that when you were a child you were badly bitten by a dog and needed to go to the hospital for stitches. A fear of dogs was immediately formed in your mind and even as you reach adulthood, you have a belief that all dogs are dangerous and will bite you - which is not necessarily true.

Emotions can serve us very well. Emotions, if intense enough, always produce behaviour. When you are in control of your emotions, they will support you in creating the life you want. This is because you will attract what is inside of you. Most people hold onto significant volumes of unprocessed negative emotions to the extent that they become a burden. They are such a burden that they affect our focus, thinking, and behaviour, producing corresponding negative results in life.

Every action you take is either fueled by love or hate. Yes, there are many other emotions such as happiness, sadness, guilt, anger, and the list goes on. If you closely examine these various emotions however, you will discover that each stems from either love or hate. Emotions push us to take action on an idea that is in our head and bring it into existence on earth. Or the emotion can cause us to NOT take action (which is also an action in itself).

Part of my coaching services is Negative Emotional Therapy[1]. Negative Emotional Therapy is a process and technique which can release a whole lifetime of unprocessed negative emotions such as anger, shame, sadness, fear, hurt, frustration, hate, doubt, anxiety, and guilt that have accumulated in your neural network over the years. It will release all the unprocessed negative emotions that have accumulated from conception until the present day. Studies[2] have shown that from the time the first cluster of cells starts to form in the mother's womb, the fetus can start to experience emotions! Maybe it's not experiencing its own emotions, but the fetus can sense the mother's emotions and accepts them as its own. This seemingly only happens if

---

1   I learnt about Negative Emotional Therapy from Burk Esterhuyse, Master Transformation Life Coach and Master Transformation Life Coach Trainer, as part of my Life Coach training course with the Transformation Coaching Academy.

2   Association for Psychological Science. «Can fetus sense mother›s psychological state? Study suggests yes.» ScienceDaily, 10 November 2011.

the mother experiences highly charged emotional events or rejects the child during pregnancy.

To date, I do not know of anything more powerful than Negative Emotional Therapy to eliminate all unprocessed negative emotions from a person's memory bank. This technique totally gets rid of a whole lifetime's worth of unprocessed emotions in a short period of time. The whole process takes about four to five hours depending on the individual. After doing Negative Emotional Therapy, a person can no longer feel emotions such as anger, shame, sadness, fear, hurt, frustration, hate, doubt, anxiety, or guilt in relation to any event that happened in their past. The memories will still be intact, but all the events will be balanced with no emotional charge left on them. This is a very powerful process and can help so many people gain control of their emotional state. As I explained earlier in this book, our emotional state determines the results that we get in life. So to change your results, you need to get in control of your emotional state.

Do you remember what I said about negative thoughts being energy in its smallest form, stored in the neural network, and connected to specific events that happened in your past? Negative Emotional Therapy releases the stored negative energy charges in a person's neural network. The process helps a person to release all of those negative emotional charges that they have built up over the years. It does not interfere with the memories themselves, it only releases the negative emotional charges.

Let me give you an example of how unprocessed negative emotions are formed in your neural network. Let us say you experienced anger for the first time in your life when you were about a year old. Maybe someone took something from you and you got angry. That was the first time in your life that you experienced anger. Your subconscious mind felt this emotion for the first time and then stored it in your neural network. After that, whenever you experienced anger, your subconscious mind would link it to the first event like a cascading chain effect. After 3-4 links the Gestalt was formed. Below is an illustration of what I mean:

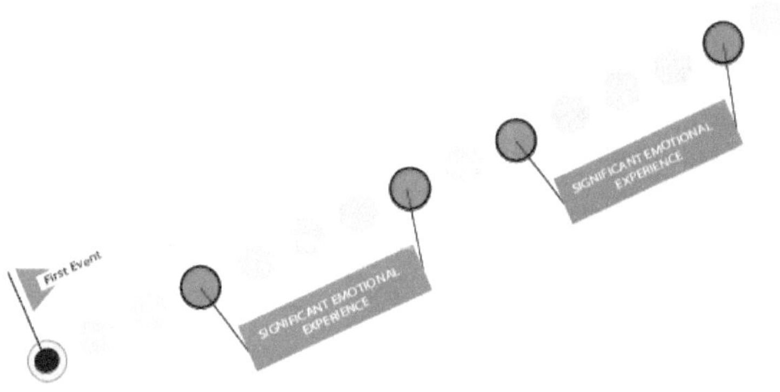

The more anger events there are in your life and the older you are, the longer the chain will become. The impact of that specific emotion gets bigger and starts controlling your life or spins it out of control when it gets triggered. What Negative Emotional Therapy does is to find the first event and then help you to deal with it by extracting lessons from it. Afterward, your subconscious will be ready to let go of the emotional charge on the event; the technique will guide you through this process of releasing the emotional charge of the first event. By letting go of the emotional charge on the first event, which was the first root for a gestalt to form in the first place, the rest of the emotional charge will release altogether. The entire gestalt (emotional chain) will collapse and the emotions will be released from the neural network. This will be done on every negative emotion, one at a time, until all of the unprocessed negative emotions are released. Then the person can no longer feel any of the above-mentioned emotions on any event that happened in their past.

Under average circumstances, talking through the negative emotions removes only the *immediate* emotion you are feeling. A lot of people have deeply rooted emotions that were triggered by a root cause event in their early ages of childhood between conception up until age 7. The Gestalt Theory mentioned above, which was developed by Fritz Perls, explains this well. Another example could be when you were 4 years old and you had an argument with your father that caused the emotion of anger in you that was not resolved. Years later a similar event happens and brings out the emotion of anger again. It makes this emotion even stronger. Years follow and the same thing happens to cause the emotion to be even deeper. And now fast forward to your current state as an adult where you experience a similar event and you are furious! You try to speak through the incident and your anger with a friend or spouse but that doesn't take away the anger - no matter how much you talk and talk and talk about it. And that is because you did not eliminate the anger from the initial root cause event. Once that root cause is addressed and the emotion linked to the root cause is tackled then you will no longer experience that same anger. Even if you experience an event similar to the root cause or any of the other events that proceeded it.

Your emotions and emotional state have a direct impact on your physiology which then affects your physical behaviours, and more especially your health due to the mind-body connection. Remember my example of how your body is upright and you have a bounce in your step when you are happy versus your body being crouched and slothful when you are sad? This is why it is crucial to always be aware of your emotional state throughout the day because your emotional state will affect how you perform tasks. You know this to be true, but what most people are not aware of is that negative emotions are not good for the body. In fact, they are the biggest cause of all our diseases and discomfort. All dark and degenerative diseases come from either a significant emotional event or due to piled-up, unprocessed negative emotions. The major negative emotions humans experience are anger, shame, sadness, fear, anxiety, frustration, doubt, hate, and guilt. Your mind will keep them in the body until it gets some type of learning or resolution to process them.

If you look at emotions from a quantum physics point of view, everything is light and energy vibrating at a certain frequency. Your emotions are energy stored up in your neural network. Negative emotions have a very low negative energy and frequency. They vibrate so low that they bring down the whole person's vibrational energy. This has a very negative effect on the person as a whole and on their health. One of the universal laws of nature is: "Like vibration attracts like vibration." A low vibratory body will attract only low vibratory things into their life. You might have wondered why so many negative things constantly happen to miserable, angry, and sad people. Their low vibration attracts all those low vibrating negative things into their lives. They are actually dying from the inside out!

The moment you release all those unprocessed negative emotions, your body's vibratory frequency will pick up. You will have a much higher vibration, thus attracting many more positive things into your life. You will have much more control over your emotions and thoughts, and you will be able to choose exactly how to feel at every moment and in every situation. Why not choose to feel great all the time? Imagine being in control of your emotions and thoughts. How much better will you be able to steer through life effortlessly? What will that be worth to you? Personally, for me, this is priceless!

There is a book titled **Power vs Force** by Dr. David R. Hawkins which speaks about how the vibrational energy within our bodies that we emit is linked to our emotions. Vibration is measured in hertz (Hz) and you vibrate higher when you are experiencing positive emotions such as happiness, love, peace, and kindness. You vibrate at lower frequencies when you experience negative emotions such as anger, hate, envy, and guilt. People who vibrate at high frequencies such as peace, which has a frequency of 600Hz, have the power to negate 10 000 000 people with frequencies of 200Hz. People such as Nelson Mandela and the great Dalai Lama are prime examples of individuals who have vibrated at such frequencies and as a result, have transformed millions of people's lives around the world.

It is crucial to emphasise that the only way to permanently remove any negative emotion which has been holding you back is through Negative Emotional Therapy. Until a point when you are ready to take part in this coaching therapy with me, you can use the below methods to temporarily eliminate negative emotions. These are not a permanent solution though. To use a metaphor, it is like continuously putting a bandage on a deep wound that keeps bleeding instead of treating the root cause of the bleed and stitching it up so that it no longer bleeds. Here are the other ways to remove negative emotions:

1. **Gratitude Journal**

   Writing a gratitude journal automatically increases your vibrations and removes any negative emotion you may be currently experiencing. Often times we focus on things that are going wrong and that is what brings about the negative emotions. Shifting your focus to something that you are grateful for immediately removes all the negative emotions and makes you happier. Appreciation is another word for gratitude, and another way to increase the positive emotion is by saying, "Thank you, thank you, thank you". Show appreciation for all the blessings in your life.

2. **Anchoring**

A technique that I do with my clients is anchoring. Anchoring is the implanting of a positive emotion in a certain place in your body, such as your wrist, which can be activated upon squeezing the area where the positive emotion is implanted. For example, I can anchor the feeling of courage or even happiness in your wrist and right before you need to stand up and say a speech in front of hundreds of people, and you are feeling nervous and anxious, you squeeze your wrist to activate these positive emotions for you to deliver a killer speech! Remember as I said earlier, the negative emotions will lead you to have a bad posture and may lead you to stutter and even back out of saying the speech. Whereas the positive emotions will fuel you to deliver an outstanding speech with a confident posture and smiling face.

When you are in control of your state you will control your results. If for some reason you are not in a resourceful state, for instance, you are feeling down, anxious, angry, hateful, or depressed, I want you to do the following: Say to yourself as loud as you can, with as much intention as possible, "I CHOOSE TO FEEL GREAT/HAPPY RIGHT NOW!" x3.

You have to emphasise as much emotion in these words as possible. Immediately afterward, think of a time when you were really happy and resourceful. Keep that thought/picture in your mind for 20 seconds and then repeat the above sentence three times again. If you do this with the mindset to succeed, you will get to that state. You <u>can</u> control your state; you just don't know it yet. You are now just like a baby, learning new things in life. The more you do this the easier it will become to reach this state. Each time will require less effort because neurons will fire together and you will as a result attract more good things in your life.

Chapter 4

WHAT'S YOUR ISSUE?

*"We cannot change what we are not aware of,
and once we are aware, we cannot help but
change."*

—Sheryl Sandberg

I absolutely love the opening quote of this chapter by Sheryl Sandberg. This quote is extremely profound; how can you change something that you're not aware of? To make it personal, how can you change something about yourself that needs alteration in order for you to obtain your desires if you're not aware that that thing needs to be changed?

In the previous chapters I spoke about how your conditioning, the way you were raised, your beliefs, your values, your attitudes, your language, your memories, and your culture are what form the filters that either delete, distort, or generalize information that you take in from the world and as a result create your reality.

So being aware of all these beliefs, conditioning, values, and cultures, and understanding the limits that all of these impose on us and on what we can truly achieve in our lives, helps us to understand the root cause of what needs to be able to change for us to live a greater life.

Firstly, you need to accept yourself and where you are now. Accept your past, what has happened to you, and the cards you have been dealt in life. Remaining angry at how badly life has treated you is only holding you back from moving forward and achieving greatness. Remember that a great future does not require a great past! You can still turn your life around and create something wonderful with it.

It's not your fault that you grew up poor or that your father was an alcoholic and abusive to you and your mother, but it is your fault if you continue to use these as excuses as to why you are not currently taking control of your life and living your best life. The power and resources you need are all inside of you at this moment, you just need to tap into them. You need to understand the power of the tools at your disposal - your conscious and subconscious mind - which will assist you in achieving your desired reality.

You need to again identify the weaknesses in all of those memories, cultures, conditioning, and attitudes that hinder you from achieving your desires – these are the **limiting beliefs**.

You must resist being trapped by how badly you were raised and your negative past experiences if you want to become that incredible person improving their relationships and achieving their career, fitness, and financial goals.

Introspection is the act of being very clear and honest with yourself and is the only way for you to identify your gaps and weaknesses in order for you to become greater. Please don't feel attacked by this exercise. Absolutely NO ONE is perfect and all of us have improvement points because all of us are not truly living the life we desire, constantly dream about, and hope for. Being genuine and true and finding out what issues you have will assist you in fixing your problems and becoming better.

Exercise:

I need you to get a pen and paper and write down the answers to the below questions. These questions will help you to identify your negative patterns, behaviours, habits, and limiting beliefs. You should set aside a minimum of 40 minutes to complete this exercise because you will need to think deeply about each question for about 1 minute to give an authentic answer that will help you resolve your issue. Ensure that you are sitting in a quiet space where you will be allowed to be alone with your thoughts and not be interrupted during this exercise.

1. Why did you choose to purchase this book and read it?
2. What is possible for you to accomplish?
3. What do you want to accomplish but find impossible to accomplish?
4. What are you capable of?
5. What are you not capable of?
6. What is your sense of self-worth?
7. What do you deserve?
8. What are your limitations?
9. So, what is the main problem?
10. How do you know you have this problem? What feelings, sights, or sounds alert you to the fact that you are experiencing this problem again?
11. When do you have this problem? And when do you not have it?
12. When did the problem start? How long have you had it?

13. Was there ever a time when you didn't have this problem?
14. What have you done to try to solve it so far?
15. What do you have to do to maintain the problem?
16. Of all the people you know, who would NEVER have this problem or any problem like this? (Real or fictional)
17. What is the difference between you and this person?
18. What stops you from being as he/she is?
19. What is your way of solving this problem?
20. What other problems do you have that are supporting and maintaining this one?

Now, I want you to pretend that you are in front of me and we are having a session in my office and that you are explaining the answers to the following questions to me:

Tafadzwa asking you: "Please teach me how to have a problem like yours?

1. What must I be thinking to have a problem like yours?
2. What story must I tell myself about my circumstances to have a problem like yours?
3. What stories must I tell myself about myself to have a problem like yours?
4. Now, what kind of mental images do I have to create or run in my mind, to have a problem like yours?
5. What kind of beliefs do I need to have, to have a problem like yours?"

Answer these questions out loud to yourself.

Examine your answers to all the above questions and take time to fully understand and notice what negative limiting beliefs have been holding you back.

IF YOUR DREAMS DON'T SCARE YOU THEN THEY ARE NOT BIG ENOUGH

"If you can dream it you can do it."

—Walt Disney

This chapter is fully an exercise because the learning is already inside you; I am merely going to help you extract it. A lot of people I speak to say they don't know what they want to do in life or what to strive for. Well, this exercise will help you solve that problem and is called "My Life's Vision" exercise.

I would like you to write down how your "Perfect Life's Vision Day" would look and feel like. There are <u>unlimited</u> hours in this day. The premise is that if you had to live a single day, over and over for eternity, and be perfectly content with it, what would it look like? Make sure to write this out in the first person, as if you are doing or living it now. Ensure that you are in an environment and state which allows you to clearly visualize all the things you will be writing down. There is no minimum or maximum time you need to take to complete this exercise, although there is a minimum number of pages you have to write. Here are some guidelines:

- It MUST be in your own handwriting. No typing out of this exercise is allowed.
- You have to have a minimum of **ten pages** written out! Very important!
- Stated in a positive present tense as if you are already living that day now.

- Money is NOT an obstacle. Imagine you have all the money you ever wanted.
- Make use of "have", "be", and "do" statements.
- Include yourself and others.
- This should be experienced every day.
- Make it descriptive, however, simple.
- Eliminate universals/generalisations.
- Use emotionally (positive) charged words.
- Everything must make you happy... Really happy.
- Remember that there is an unlimited amount of hours in this day.

Here are some additional questions to help you write out your "Perfect Life's Vision Day". Be as specific as possible in the answers:

1. Where do you live?
2. What kind of bed and bedroom are you waking up in?
3. Who do you wake up next to?
4. How is your relationship with this person?
5. How do you feel about yourself and your life?
6. What positive empowering self-talk is going on in your head?
7. How much do you love yourself and your life?
8. How are your health and energy levels?
9. How creative are you?
10. What does your house look like? How big is your house?
11. What do you do in the morning?
12. With whom do you have breakfast?

13.   What are you thinking and talking about?

14.   What vehicles do you drive?

15.   Where do you spend the first half of the day? What do you get up to in the morning?

16.   What is your business or career about? It must be something you really love to do!

17.   What do you actually do in your business or career?

18.   What kind of employees or colleagues do you have?

19.   What are your clients like?

20.   With whom do you have lunch? What do you talk about?

21.   What are your friends like?

22.   What do you do for personal fulfilment?

23.   What life purpose are you striving towards?

24.   What is your relationship like with your spouse? Family? Friends?

25.   What do you do for family time?

26.   Where do you eat dinner?

27.   Who do you eat with? What do you talk about?

28.   What time do you go to bed?

29.   What does that look like?

30.   What do you think about when you go to bed and what do you do just before you fall asleep?

Once you have completed your "Perfect Life's Vision Day" exercise on paper, I want you to get onto the internet or get some magazines and find pictures & symbols that represent your "Life's Vision". Start to create a "Vision Board" that represents your "Life's Vision". Hang that board on the wall in front of your bed and look at it every day and know that THIS life is already yours! Remember that you are the ARCHITECT OF YOUR LIFE! Make sure you look at the vision board every day! The visuals that your brain takes in daily when looking at your vision board will become deeply embedded in your subconscious mind which will result in your subconscious attracting the things you desire into your life.

Chapter 6

WHAT IS YOUR END GOAL?

"Without dreams and goals there is no living, only merely existing, and that is not why we are here."

—Mark Twain

Okay so now you've reached the halfway mark of this book and the reason why you even purchased it in the first place is that there is something that you desired to transform in your life. Regardless of whether it's your physical body that you want to transform because you want a better physique, or maybe relationship-wise you want to improve the relationship with your children or with your spouse. Perhaps it's your career or business goal that you want to transform and improve and take to the next level or into a completely new trajectory. Whatever your goal may be, no matter what it is, I have a guiding system that can assist and ensure you achieve your goal!

The more and more people I meet and coach the more I have come to learn that the majority of people in the world do not even set goals for themselves! They don't set goals because of a variety of reasons. The main ones that they admit to me are either:

- fear that they will fail;
- fear and self-doubt that they are not good enough and;
- fear of living outside of their comfort zone.

I will cover tools on how to overcome fear and self-doubt in the coming chapters but in this chapter, I will speak more on the few people who attempt to set goals and set out to achieve them.

The biggest problem that people experience when it comes to achieving their goals is that the moment they think of their goals they view them as a gigantic and overwhelming mountain to conquer, and they become scared and intimidated by said goals. They begin to think, "Wow! How on earth am I going to achieve this goal? It requires an incredible amount of work!" And at this point, they get paralysed by fear and don't even attempt the first step towards their goal. There is a saying that goes: "If your dreams don't scare you then they are not big enough". I agree with it wholeheartedly! You need to dream big! There is literally NOTHING that you can't achieve in life. Do not put limitations on your dreams and your goals because of the conditioning and limiting beliefs you were raised with, as I mentioned in Chapter 2. You were created as a powerful being destined for greatness and if you don't live your best life then you are wasting your life playing small which will serve absolutely no one. Live your best life and let your light shine! The world needs your purpose to be lived out.

The trick to achieving this enormous goal is to just break it down into smaller goals and not make it such a big task which you must complete ALL at once. That is actually how you achieve your goals: bit by bit, small step by small step. It is about achieving every single small step with excellence and consistency (which I will cover in Chapter 11) and then after a certain amount of time if you look back and take in all the work you have done you will see that you would have achieved your goal; if not, you will notice that you are at the brink of achieving it!

It is crucial that you break down your goal into time frame intervals such as three years, one year, six months, three months, and then one month. Once at the one-month interval, you can break it up into weeks and then into daily goals.

The next step is to make sure you really have a desire for what you want to have or whatever it is that you want to set a goal towards. In the book called **Think and Grow Rich** by Napoleon Hill, the first chapter after the introduction talks about desire and how every single goal and success story starts with someone having a deep desire for something. And when I say desire I don't mean you just *like* something or are *kind of* interested in achieving something. I mean you REALLY want to fulfil this goal and when things get tough you're not going to give up and quit the process! The desire will push you through and keep you self-disciplined and will keep you motivated to keep on doing the work. So make sure you genuinely want what you're seeking to achieve and that it's not just for the hype or the clout nor the social media likes. It's something that you really, really want in your life.

Next, you need to be very specific and include detail when you write down your goal. Write down your goal in a sentence and be specific. A lot of us are not very specific and actually end up not achieving our goals because we were not specific enough. For example, if you want to lose weight state your ideal weight and say I want to lose 10 kg so that I can be 65 kg. Only vaguely saying "I want to lose weight" is not sufficient. You could lose only 1 kg and that would classify as you achieving your goal but we all know there is way more that you need to lose.

As you write your goal out be sure to do so in the present tense starting with today's date, and the statement, "I'm so happy"; then state your goal, and write down, "Thank you, thank you, thank you". For example:

"It is (Date)… and I am so happy now that…
(state specific goal, in the present tense,
starting with 'I have…' or 'I am…' or 'I allow myself to…').
Thank you, Thank you, Thank you."

OR

"I am so happy now that…
(state specific goal, in the present tense,
starting with 'I have…' or 'I am…' or 'I allow myself to…').
Thank you, Thank you, Thank you."

You need to write it down in the present tense because like I mentioned in the first chapter your subconscious doesn't know truth from a lie so now it believes that you are telling it a "truth" (even though it may not currently be true). For example, "I currently earn $50 000 per month". Your goal may not be true now, but because of the vast power of your subconscious, it will attract this goal into your life until it becomes your truth and reality!

Next up is to put a daily plan of action in place. Earlier you would have broken down your goal from three years to 1 year, then to 6 months, and eventually 1 month. You will now break it down into smaller chunks - weekly and then daily. After successful completion of your daily goals, you'll see that after 7 days you would have done a week's worth of work! And after completing 4 cycles of 7 days you would have achieved a whole month's worth of work! Then after successfully and consistently completing six cycles of those one-month goals you would have achieved 6 months' worth of your goal! Did you know that if you consistently work hard for 6 months then you will put yourself FIVE years ahead of so many other people who would have literally spent their 6 months doing nothing more with their lives than just going with the flow and not taking any action to pursue their dreams?! So utilize 6 months; it's a lot of time to make a big difference within your life!

Write down your goals on a piece of paper every single day for 7 to 21 days so that they actually get embedded in your subconscious mind. As stated in Chapter 1, the subconscious mind is programmed through repetition! A classic example is the Times/Multiplication Table. Without even thinking long about it, if I ask you what 3 multiplied by 3 is, you will automatically say 9. If I ask what 10 multiplied by 5 is, you will automatically say 50. However, if I ask you what 13 multiplied by 14 is you won't be able to automatically tell me. That is because growing up our teachers taught us the multiplication table only up until number 12 and anything above that requires a calculator. We learnt these through constant repetition on a daily basis for a good couple of months until they were deeply embedded in our subconscious mind and as a result, we will literally never forget them. We learnt the multiplication table that way and it is something we will never forget because it is programmed into our subconscious mind, so it's crucial to make sure you do the same with your goals for your subconscious mind to help you achieve them.

After writing down your goal every day for 21 days, write it down on a small cardboard paper and laminate it. Carry that laminated, compact cardboard with you everywhere you go! Make sure you look at it daily and if possible, make sure you look at it first thing in the morning when you wake up. This is the process of embedding it into your subconscious mind. Carry that laminated paper in your pocket or handbag and make sure that you're always reading it and saying it out loud. Feel the positive emotions surging through your body that come with reading out that goal, and allow yourself to experience the feeling of appreciation of having achieved the goal. Let yourself feel the positive emotions flowing through your body when you envision the goal.

Remember that you must never give up, never give in! I will not lie to you; things are going to get tough during the process of achieving your goal but what you need to do is to keep on going and persevering! You will also need to be patient with the goal and give it time to come to fruition. There is no such thing as instant gratification when it comes to goals. Great things take time to achieve. You don't just plant a seed today then expect a huge tree to have fully grown by tomorrow. Growth takes time and you need to be self-disciplined which will be covered in Chapter 9.

You need to be committed to making sure that even when the going gets tough, you're dedicated to achieving this goal and you won't ever quit! Faith is extremely important in achieving your goal because while working towards it you are putting effort into something that you haven't even seen yet. Faith requires you to believe in something that you haven't seen or can't see yet but that you know in your heart WILL come to fruition without a doubt.

And lastly, you need to have focus. Remain focused on your goal and don't allow yourself to be distracted by the many distractions that are in the world. There are a lot of social media apps out there to keep you busy and distracted for hours on end and that can eat up all the time that could be used to progress towards your goals, which you will never get back. Keep your focus and you will most certainly be able to achieve your goal.

FEAR - FALSE EVIDENCE APPEARING REAL

"Being brave isn't the absence of fear. Being brave is having that fear but finding a way through it."

—Bear Grylls

When it comes to setting goals there is a well-known strategy. The strategy states that you should make SMART goals:

> **S** – Specific
> **M** – Measurable
> **A** – Attainable
> **R** – Realistic
> **T** – Time-based

I agree with 80% of this strategy and I will explain why. Yes, goals must be specific; you need to be as detailed as possible as to how this goal looks and how it will be achieved because being vague or general will have you following useless directions towards what you think you need to achieve, but which will lead you further away from your true goal.

Yes, goals must be measurable; you need a way to measure your progress to assess if you are growing closer to your goal or not. For example, during your weight loss journey, you start a new diet which will lead to you shedding off some kilograms and to assess its effectiveness you check how many kilograms you have lost after a month on this diet. The number of kilograms lost is the measurement you will use to assess whether that specific diet is working for you and if you are closer to reaching your goal or not.

Yes, your goals must be attainable. I think this goes without saying that OF COURSE your goals are attainable or else you wouldn't have had the vision of this goal in the first place. There is a reason why God put this vision/goal inside you. It is the purpose you are meant to fulfil on this earth even if it is to bake cakes every day! Every purpose in this world has its place. I want to emphasize that your vision is inside you! Meaning that other people won't see it or understand it until it manifests in the outside world and is a success. So please do not be discouraged when other people, even family and friends, don't support you from the get-go and/or think your dream or vision is unattainable or absurd to pursue until they start seeing physical results themselves. It's funny how the doubters all of a sudden become your biggest fans once you have achieved what you have been trying to tell them consistently before that you **will** achieve. Keep believing in the dream and vision inside you. It WILL manifest!

And yes, goals must be time-based because a goal without a scheduled time of completion is just a dream and I strongly oppose anyone who stays trapped in the fantasy of achieving their goals in their heads and never takes action but only procrastinates executing tasks due to repeated excuses.

What I do not agree with, however, is that goals needing to be realistic. Notice how by dimming down the goal you are already revealing that you believe that there is a limit to what you can achieve. We all have dreams and goals that we want to achieve. The bigger the dream, the better, because there is no such thing as unrealistic. You can achieve ANYTHING you set your mind to if you back it up with hard work, consistency, and the various other factors I discuss in this book.

I know the thought of an "unrealistic" goal is very daunting to even fathom, let alone start doing the work towards, but trust me - if your dreams/goals don't scare you, then they are not big enough!

Being scared of this goal means that there is a fear inside of you that is preventing you from achieving your goal, resulting in paralysis and thus stopping you from taking action. There are many different forms that this fear will manifest itself such as the following:

- Fear of failure that something will go wrong and you will not achieve your goal.
- Fear of what others will say or think about you when you pursue this goal.
- Fear of success in that if you do manage to achieve this goal will you be able to handle the responsibilities or all the fame that comes with this goal?
- Fear of the unknown because taking action towards this goal is pushing you out of your comfort zone into unknown and unfamiliar territory.

This is not an exhaustive list because there are many more ways that this fear can manifest. Regardless of whichever type of fear you are experiencing, it is important to take the leap of faith and dive headfirst into pursuing your dream or goal!

One of my coaching service offerings is coaching in Public Speaking and the main reason that most of my clients give me for not being able to speak in public is that they fear standing up in front of a crowd or their colleagues and forgetting their words. They are afraid of making a fool of themselves or that no one will be interested in what they are saying. Them speaking has not even happened yet but they have already thought of one hundred scenarios in their mind of all the things that COULD go wrong which leads to them being paralysed to take action in the first place. Instead of focusing on what can go wrong, rather focus on what can go RIGHT. Remember how the subconscious mind works; it manifests what you tell it. You get what you focus on; so rather focus on what you want to get! If you focus on the negative outcome, you will surely attract that negative outcome.

On the other side of fear are breakthroughs and successes. Action in spite of fear is what separates average humans from the legends and winners people aspire to be like and look up to. Fear is the reason why the graveyard is so rich with million-dollar businesses that were never started because people were too scared to pursue their ideas. If it were not for fearless individuals such as Nelson Mandela that led the fight against the fall of apartheid and the liberation of black people in South Africa in 1994, then where would black people be now in South Africa? To be great you need to show courage and courage is not the absence of fear but action despite fear. Successful people have fears too. They just don't let their fears stop them.

Here are a few practical steps to assist you in taking action despite fear:

1.   ***Identify the Fear and Face It***

I had mentioned a few fears earlier in this chapter to illustrate what types of fear creep up when someone wants to achieve their goal. Sit down and be honest with yourself and pinpoint which exact fear is holding you back. Once you have identified that fear, find weaknesses in that fear by questioning its basis and also minimising the size of the fear to not be as big as you perceive it to be. When my clients tell me that they want to be a millionaire but they fear that they will not achieve this goal because it is very difficult to achieve, I give them the example of how currently there are 46.8 million people who are millionaires in the world but only 5,294 people, as at January 2019, have climbed Mount Everest. You can Google this, it's actually true. So that means it's easier to become a millionaire than to climb Mount Everest! That thought process helped me to see that becoming a millionaire is not as daunting as it is in my head. God has placed the best things in life on the other side of fear, so face your fear!

2. **Prepare, Practice, and Role Play**

They say that practice makes perfect so if your goal is linked to a certain event that you are looking towards, but you are anxious about how it will play out, then practice it in your head first. For example, if it is public speaking and you need to say a speech in front of an audience then spend a few nights before the event standing in front of your mirror saying your speech and working on your body posture and movements, word for word, and movement by movement. When the day arrives, all you have to do is play out everything you have been practicing which will flow out of you effortlessly.

Here is a tip when it comes to public speaking: 50% of the audience will be responsive and the other 50% will not. Do not focus on the 50% that are not laughing at your jokes or nodding at every one of your powerful insight points. This will throw you off your game and you will forget your words, stutter, and lose composure. Simply focus on that one individual in the crowd that is nodding at you and giving you their warm smile. They will be the key to you getting through your speech without panic.

3.   **Ask for Guidance/Assistance**

The fear of the unknown is quite a legitimate one because you don't know what you don't know, so how will you know what to avoid and be cautious of? The thought that the next action you take towards your goal could be detrimental to you achieving it causes multiple heart palpitations. In this scenario, it is always crucial to have a mentor or coach to help and guide you along your path. Your mentor or coach is someone that has travelled the road that you are looking to also walk down and has expertise in the field or industry that your goal lies in. An example would be a fitness coach if you are looking to get a healthier body or a business coach if you are looking to become an entrepreneur and start your own company. Having someone there with you helping you and guiding you quickly eliminates all fear of the unknown because you have someone you trust showing you the ropes.

Exercise:

1.   Write down the fear that is holding you back from starting to work on your dream:

____

____

____

2. Write down why this fear is not as big as it seems:

____

____

____

3. Who can help you along the way in achieving this goal so that you do not have to go through the journey alone?:

____

____

____

Chapter 8

THE INVISIBLE GIANT - ANXIETY

"Anxiety is nothing...
but repeatedly re-experiencing failure in
advance. What a waste."

—Seth Godin

In Chapter 1 I spoke about how one of the prime directives of the conscious mind is that it is time-bound; meaning that it avoids the now. It focuses predominantly on the past and the future. When it focuses on past events that have already taken place in your life, emotions such as guilt, self-pity, and regret come up. When it focuses on future events that have not even happened yet, emotions such as worry, anxiety, doubt, and fear come up.

Anxiety and worry have become one of the biggest causes of depression in today's time. We are anxious because of our jobs that require us to work insane hours to meet unreasonable deadlines and report to ungrateful and rude managers. We are anxious because getting into a committed and long-term relationship has become a challenging and an almost near-death experience to attempt in this generation where hookups are the norm, and where no one is trying to get into anything serious because they are waiting for the next best thing to come along. We are anxious because we see pictures on social media of people living what we assume are "perfect" lives for the reason that we see them in their expensive clothes posing next to expensive cars and going on extravagant holidays with the love of their life. And then we make the mistake of allowing our mind to play the comparison game and we compare ourselves to what we see on social media. You see that you are single, still living at home, and working at a job that drains your soul and doesn't even afford you the opportunity to go on a nice international holiday once a year.

We get anxious because our health is in poor condition as brought on by the fact that we maintain poor eating habits, that healthy food is expensive, and we have a lack of time to exercise at least 3 times a week in between our busy schedules. We worry if we will even see ourselves reach age 70 and not need a wheelchair to move around in. We get anxious when we are uncertain about what tomorrow holds and based on what we see on the news because it's never good. The world is in turmoil because of gender-based violence, racism, retrenchments, murders, global warming, and the list goes on and on. All this negativity plays in our minds unconsciously and we expect the worst to happen to us just when we simply walked out the door.

As I write this book currently it is July 2020 and there is a pandemic known as the Novel Coronavirus (Covid-19) plaguing every nation in the world. We are currently worried about the health and safety of our loved ones and ourselves as well as job security due to numerous businesses being shut down because they were not able to perform in this tough economic environment. They say that the greatest form of wealth in this current time is now a peace of mind and I agree. If you have inner peace and do not constantly feel anxious then you are truly blessed.

Clearly, there are a LOT of things to tackle that bring on anxiety and worry but to keep it in line with the theme of transforming your subconscious mind to achieve your goals, I will focus on the anxiety relating to your goals. Although I do believe that the principles can be applied to any specific topic that brings you anxiety.

Firstly, you need to accept that there are things that you can control or change and there are things that you cannot control or change. Anxiety mainly comes in when we want to change or control a certain situation or future outcome but there is nothing we can do about it. We then worry about how things will turn out. That needs to stop as of today. Accept the things that you cannot change and learn to not hold onto thoughts of what could happen or not happen because no matter how much you stress and worry there is literally nothing you can do about it. Your worrying, stressing, and sleepless nights will not change the outcome so you might as well drink a cup of chamomile tea, go to bed and get a good night's rest. I love the serenity prayer because it gives great guidance on how to handle situations that we can and cannot change. The prayer goes: "God, grant me the serenity to accept the things I cannot change, courage to change the things I can and wisdom to know the difference." Don't let anxiety about what you cannot change stop you from living a happy and peaceful life.

At the core of it all, anxiety is simply your conscious mind worrying about a future event that hasn't happened yet. A lot of people even experience panic attacks just from worrying and stressing about something that hasn't happened yet. When you start to feel that panic coming and getting stronger within you, you need to act fast and bring yourself back to the present moment! You can do this through grounding exercises or even breathing exercises.

Grounding and Breathing Exercises

Grounding is a technique where you bring your focus to the current reality. You can do this in various ways but the most common is removing your shoes and going outside to your garden, placing both feet on the grass, closing your eyes, and breathing in and out. You can even hold onto a tree because the aim is to connect with nature and calm yourself down.

A common technique to alleviate your anxiety is also breathing exercises. When you experience anxiety, I am sure you have noticed that your breathing gets short and quick and your heartbeat gets faster. It is because your body has now gone into "fight or flight mode" as a reaction to the thoughts of disaster or negativity of the future event that hasn't even happened yet. Controlling your breathing will help you to slow down your heartbeat to a calm state so that your body does not feel tense and anxious. I normally recommend the 1 to 2 ratio of breathing. In other words, breathe in slowly for 2 seconds, then slowly exhale for 4 seconds. Or breathe in slowly for 3 seconds then slowly exhale for 6 seconds and so on and so forth. Do this until you feel your body becoming calm and your heartbeat returning to its normal state.

Speak to Someone You Trust

A huge reliever of anxiety is speaking to someone that you trust to be vulnerable with in sharing your anxious thoughts in order to eliminate them. This is because 9 times out of 10 the thoughts you are thinking are probably extremely exaggerated. I know from personal experience that I used to be a victim of this. I would always think of the worst possible outcome that could occur which gave me anxiety and stress! But then when I shared my thoughts with someone that I trusted I would continually get to the realisation that what I was fearing would happen would most likely not happen and that things weren't as bad as what I was making them out to be. It's incredible how the mind works; it's creative and your imagination can be your best friend but also your worst enemy. So, it's crucial that you learn to control the thoughts that go through your mind. Do not allow the negative thoughts to win and paralyse you with anxiety in your current reality.

Meditation and Prayer

Meditation and prayer are extremely effective ways to eliminate anxiety. If you are religious or spiritual, then you will resonate with the word prayer because that is how you communicate to your Creator or the Higher Power which you connect to and draw strength from. Anxiety comes from a disconnect between you and your Higher Power and a lack of belief in the goodness that has been promised to you from Them.

Prayer helps you to reconnect with the purpose that your Creator has for you and reminds you that you will live a life of abundance and blessings. Therefore, you should not fear or be anxious about anything because you are protected! Meditation is more of a spiritual practice where you calm the mind and calm your thoughts. There are many guided meditations that are excellent and I personally use them when I want to fall asleep at night. I can't even count on two hands how many times I have fallen asleep during meditation because my mind and body become so relaxed that by the time I am halfway through the guided meditation, I fall asleep like a baby.

Exercise

Exercise, exercise, exercise! The body automatically releases endorphins when you exercise and these are natural hormones that make you happy, elevate your mood, and relieve anxiety. After a good workout, you will immediately feel better inside and experience less stress. The cherry on top is that by the time your head hits the pillow that evening, you are guaranteed a good night's rest.

Chapter 9

MASTER YOURSELF, MASTER THE WORLD!

"You will never always be motivated. So, you have to learn to be disciplined."

—Unknown

We have all heard the saying that goes: "Discipline will get you from where you are now, to achieving your goals". We all agree with it and we all nod vehemently when we hear it… but the difficult part comes when we actually need to DO it! Putting in the work for the first couple of days is the easy part, but being disciplined enough to do the work consistently, especially on days where you just don't feel like doing the work, is extremely tough and takes a lot of sacrifice.

That dreaded word: "Self-discipline"! A hard pill that we all struggle to swallow but truth be told, if we all applied self-discipline to every aspect of our lives, we would not be miserable. Humans are not machines who can do the same task at the same time every day without fail and at the push of a button. Some humans love to relax and partake in spontaneity, so self-discipline tends to feel like a chore or even boring after a while. It's because of this nature in humans that we all admire people who have immense self-discipline. Think about it. Why do we love watching the Olympics, World Cups, or any other competitive sport? We love to watch people compete for the top prize and become number 1 through consistent practice and training to obtain a championship or an award-winning level, which can only be attained through… self-discipline.

This concept is true for any person we look up to as successful. We admire top businessmen and businesswomen because they have achieved great success as a result of their incredible work ethic and self-discipline. Sexual temptation is always around us but successful long-term marriages stem from two partners being self-disciplined enough to commit to one person for the rest of their life and never derailing from that.

The (not so) secret ingredient to making your desires a reality is self-discipline and the sooner you start implementing that in your life, the sooner you will be successful.

I'm sure in your mind you are now eagerly waiting for me to reveal to you what the key is to unlocking the self-discipline power within you. Well, unfortunately, I can't give you self-discipline or teach it to you; it has to come from you, hence it is called _self_-discipline. Believe it or not, we all have the self-discipline power inside of us; the important thing is to tap into and activate it.

Here are a few methods to get you into the routine of self-discipline until it becomes a habit and second nature where you don't have to try as hard to force yourself to perform certain actions:

1.   Create the Right Environment

I want you to imagine yourself as a person who is obsessed with snacking and your goal is to lose weight. You have noticed that one of the main contributors to your excessive weight is because you eat a lot of junk food daily. If you have a cupboard in your kitchen packed with crisps, sweets, chocolates, and fizzy drinks you will be incapable of losing the weight you desire because every time you walk into your kitchen and open your cupboard to fetch something to cook you will see those snacks and get tempted to eat them. Something is most likely to happen when you are feeling slightly hungry or peckish and you want to have something to eat but don't have the energy to cook a proper nutritional meal. You will automatically head over to your snack cupboard and start digging into the first packet of crisps you see, right?

At this point, your goal will be postponed until the day you decide to take control and stop snacking on junk food. The main reason for your downfall here is because the right environment to promote healthy eating was not created. Creating the right environment for you to achieve your goal means removing anything that will hinder you from moving closer to your goal and replacing those things with things that will propel you forward towards obtaining your goal. In this example, you would then remove all the unhealthy junk food from your cupboard then replace them with healthy snacks such as fruit and plant-based food which can be prepared into healthy snacks to consume.

A drug addict that wants to quit cannot continuously hang out in the same dingy park where the drug lords hang out and the drug addicts take hits of their narcotics, and still expect to walk away without falling into the temptation of taking the drugs themself. You need a new environment that will not remind you of the old behaviours that you are trying to leave behind. To become a new version of yourself you will require a new environment for your new self. If you get a house plant as a gift and you want it to grow, you do not put it in a dark place and only water it and expect it to grow. No, you need to take it out of the dark environment and expose it to sunlight plus water it, and only <u>then</u> will it grow.

I know some will want to challenge this and say true self-discipline is being put in the old environment and having the strength and self-discipline to say NO to those temptations. I agree 100% with you. That is indeed true self-discipline. However, that only occurs once this new behaviour has become a habit, after the initial stages when you are first making the adjustments in your life and training your body to let go of the unhealthy, unwanted, and old habits that would offer the temptation to relapse into old patterns. This needs to be done for at least 21 days.

2.   Learn to Say No to Self

As humans, we all have vices and carnal cravings that prevent us from becoming the best version of ourselves. A common example is oversleeping or wanting to relax all the time. Your body and flesh don't always want to put in the work and with this new generation we live in of instant gratification, more and more of us are extremely lazy to put in continuous work. Yet, we expect everything to be given to us NOW with no work from our side. Most of the time you will not feel like putting in the work and discipline needed to complete a task and your body will literally be screaming at you saying, "Just relax. You've already put in so much work. Why are you working so hard? Let's just relax and sleep. We aren't seeing any results anyway". This voice tends to come up too often and most people fall for it. They end up listening and don't engage in that exercise workout or finishing that business proposal which could be used to get funding for their venture, or even putting in that extra effort with their spouse to improve their relationship. And that is why your life remains the same: the miserable, boring, and half-lived life it has always been. Because you did not learn to say no to self and push yourself when the time needed you to step up!

Discipline has received a bad name because most people think of it as punishment. Discipline is the foregoing of immediate pleasure for the exchange of long-term self-respect. Self-discipline means self-love. So, if you say you love yourself that means you engage in behaviours towards yourself that are loving. You cannot win the war against the world when you cannot even win the war within your mind and body.

3.   Create a Routine

I love the fact that our body learns and even has a "body clock". Have you ever noticed that if you set your alarm for work to 6 am every day for about a month or two, and one night your phone accidentally dies because you forgot to charge it, the next morning you automatically wake up at 6 am even without your alarm? That was your body clock working for you.

Getting your body used to a certain routine at a certain daily time will help you with your self-discipline because your body will start automatically getting used to a particular action happening at a certain time without you even putting any conscious effort into it. Growing up my parents would always make us switch the TV off at 7 pm and we all had to sit at the dining room table and either do our homework or read a book if we did not have any homework. This was a daily routine for us as kids and because of that upbringing I now have the self-discipline to come home from work every night and be productive in the evenings where I work on my business or I read a book. A lot of people see me as a person with a lot of self-discipline and a great work ethic but for me, it's just how my body operates because that is how my parents raised me. I don't even think too hard about it; it's become normalised.

4.   Find a Motivator or an Inspiration

When you don't feel like executing your tasks or don't feel in the mood for it, you should always think of something that will motivate or inspire you to do it. If you are aiming for a fitness goal, for example, have a picture of the body type you desire to have on your Vision Board (Refer to Chapter 5).

5.   Get an Accountability Partner

There is a saying that goes: "Being lazy and not achieving your goals is an insult to those that believe in you". This saying hits me hard every time I read it and makes me want to push myself towards achieving my goals, not only to avoid letting myself down but also my family and friends who continuously encourage me and want the best for me. Tell your goals to someone, or a group of people, that will hold you accountable for the progress of your endeavours towards your goals. Most people are afraid to tell anyone their goals because of the fear that they won't achieve them and will be embarrassed, and will appear as a failure. Don't let that fear consume you. Rather do the opposite. Use the fear that you might fail in front of your friends and family as motivation to ensure that you <u>don't</u> fail! Remember that fear can also be used to drive action if you use it correctly instead of it causing you to freeze and not take action.

A simple example of accountability is if you want to lose weight and get fit; join a running club or a gym workout group and exchange numbers with the people in the group so that you can send each other reminders on WhatsApp to workout, or send motivation to each other when you are feeling down and demotivated.

Chapter 10

THE ONLY THING HOLDING YOU BACK IS YOU!

"Self-doubt kills talent."

—Edie McClurg

A sad truth about us humans is that while growing up, and as a result of the negative experiences we have experienced in life, we all end up developing a sense of, "I am not worthy", or, "I am not good enough". It creeps in at the worst of times which then holds us back from achieving something. These feelings normally stem from a root cause event that occurred between the age of when you were conceived and forming in your mother's womb to the age of 7. Any traumatic or negative event that you went through brought on the negative feeling of rejection or sadness and thus resulted in forming the limiting belief that you are "not worthy" or "not good enough" to receive a certain thing. <u>All</u> clients that I have worked with have a limiting belief of not being worthy or good enough. The root event results in numerous limiting beliefs as an adult such as not being good enough to excel in their career, that they are not worthy of finding a true love partner or that they are not worthy of owning wealth, amongst others.

I coach my clients in my one-on-one sessions to confront this root event and eliminate the negative emotion and limiting belief that is charged so that the event no longer holds them back. I coach this therapy based on a technique called *Time-Line Theory* which is a powerful therapeutic process that has evolved from hypnosis and Neuro-Linguistic Programming (NLP) developed by Tad James, Ph.D., in the 1980s. Remember that to permanently remove a limiting belief and negative emotion is to eliminate the negative emotion and limiting belief attached to a root event.

It is most likely that you are reading this book because you have not been able to start any one-on-one coaching sessions with me but would like to start your journey of transformation until you are ready to start with your coaching sessions. Here are more techniques for you to incorporate as part of your behaviours which will aid you in eliminating self-doubt until we can work together to permanently eliminate the behaviours:

1.   Create a New Self-Image

Traumatic and negative events that occur in our lives lead us to put our guard up when it comes to a certain topic and we form a "protective" barrier around ourselves that actually works against us and not FOR us. For example, as a child, you got allocated a role to perform in a school play and when it was show night, your time came up to speak but at that moment you went completely blank and forgot all your lines. You ran off the stage crying, and kids teased you for weeks on end and never let you forget what an epic fail you were and how embarrassing the moment was. This event will negatively impact you to the point where you become a shy child who doesn't like putting themselves out there. You grow up with the self-image of being "shy" until you become an adult and are part of the working class, and you avoid speaking in the boardroom in front of board members or even at a townhall at work because you are too "shy". Truth be told, you are not shy. You just have a negative self-image of being shy and that is what you end up projecting to the world. The perception you have about yourself is exactly what you are projecting to the outside world.

In summary, your perception = Your self-image = "You are who you think you are".

Our perception is what we are programmed/condition-ed to see about ourselves. The world will always treat you according to your perception of yourself, so it is crucial that you have a positive self-image in order to transform yourself. You cannot expect the mirror to smile first. Watch how quickly your life transforms once you stop telling yourself negative things about yourself and start telling yourself positive things about yourself. What matters most is how you see yourself as depicted in the illustration below:

2.   Tell Yourself Positive Affirmations Daily

One of my favourite affirmations is, "I am brilliant. I am bright. I am a radiant being of light. I'm an outstanding peak performer. I'm a dynamic life transformer." I learnt these affirmations from Robin Banks who is an extremely energetic speaker on "Mind Power". I always use these words whenever I am asked for what I want a host or moderator to present as my introduction, and it has also formed part of my biography for this book! The words are extremely positive and hype me up with extreme confidence which I use to deliver impactful and energetic coaching sessions with clients or during an interview. Before I go out and put myself out there as a successful and impactful life coach, I have to continuously engage in positive self-talk that I AM a successful and positive life coach. Imagine if I kept saying to myself, "I am shy and I am not confident". I would most likely not be that great of a life coach. If I even dared to approach anyone with the concept of life coaching in the first place, I most probably wouldn't have any impact on their life.

At first, these affirmations may seem like lies about yourself because they are not yet a current reality. For example, telling yourself "I am a wealthy entrepreneur" when you only started your business a week ago. That is absolutely fine. Remember from Chapter 1 that your subconscious does not know the difference between the truth and a lie and it will believe whatever you are telling it and will eventually manifest what you repeatedly say to it. So, make sure you are telling it positivity all the time. Make sure your affirmations are short and catchy so that they are easy to say and absorb.

3.   Stop Comparing Yourself to Other People

In this age of the internet and social media including Facebook and Instagram, it has become so easy for us to share our lives with anyone around the world and keep up to date with our favourite celebrities. There has also been an increase in depression amongst society. This is as a result of people comparing their seemingly *boring, uneventful,* and *poor* life with the lives of people posting the most "amazing" pictures of themselves in designer label clothes standing next to expensive cars, and going on extravagant holidays in exotic locations with the love of their lives who they got married to a few months ago.

We constantly see these images and start to unconsciously think that we are not worthy of the same blessings because we have not been blessed with success as yet. After prolonged comparison to filtered pictures of "perfection", we start to believe that we are not capable of achieving the same thing, if not more! And we then start doubting the path we have chosen to pursue because we look at how "great and successful" someone else's path has turned out for them, while we are still waiting for our breakthrough that hasn't happened despite putting in an endless effort. Worse yet, we see no results regardless of how hard we are working. This leads to self-doubt and the belief that success will not find us, but in due time, it will! You need to just stay in your lane and keep focused on your own life and your values or goals as well as your definition of success. Never allow other people's pictures of their lives to make you feel less than who you really are.

4. How Someone Treats You is Not Because You Are a Bad Person

We all experience stress and trauma in our lives and most people project this stress and trauma onto people as a reaction to their personal stress and trauma. Many people allow other people's negative behaviours towards them make them feel less about themselves. It's important to never internalize someone else's negative behaviours towards you. For example, you apply for a job at a company you have always been wanting to work for. You prepare for weeks for the interview and you feel confident and competent for the job. You then attend the interview and the interviewer is rude, condescending, and continually interrupts you while you try to answer the interview questions. They never allow you to fully answer a question and what makes things worse is the reaction on their face is one of being unimpressed.

This interview leaves you feeling incompetent and as though you are not worthy of such a position in a company of your dreams! If you knew the truth that the reason the interview was so bad was not that you were incompetent but because the interviewer was having a bad day due to problems at home with their spouse and having been involved in a car accident with a taxi, for which the costs to repair would be extensive, you may have a different perspective. Don't personalize other people's behaviours. What someone does, most of the time, has absolutely nothing to do with you! People are very complex and have a lot of things going on that you might not actually understand or even know about. Don't internalize fleeting behaviours and emotions. Stop blaming yourself! Always aim to not let external factors affect your emotional state.

Exercise:

Write a list describing your new self-image. Write down a list of ten words or ten short sentences of no more than 4 four words each. For the next 30 days in the morning and evenings, repeat that list to yourself out loud in a confident voice and feel the feelings that are associated with that new self-image. Also, ensure that you see yourself as this new self-image. The picture of you should be bright and colourful and the image should be you achieving your goal.

Chapter 11:

CONSISTENCY IS KEY!

"The hallmark of excellence, the test of greatness, is consistency".

—Jim Tressel

I am a qualified chartered accountant by profession and one interesting concept we all learn in university as accounting students is the principle of the compound interest effect. Compound interest is interest calculated on the initial principal amount, which also includes all of the accumulated interest from previous periods on a deposit or loan. In simple terms, this means compound interest is "interest on interest" meaning interest on the principal amount, as well as interest on the previous interest amounts that have accumulated. This is versus simple interest which is only interest calculated on the principal amount. Compound interest, therefore, makes the sum of the amount grow at a much faster rate compared to simple interest.

I strongly believe that the compound interest effect can also be applied to daily life as well in order to achieve a certain goal at a much faster rate. Doing a little extra than normal will result in greater results in the long term. This is because of the compound interest effect. I will refer to the below image to illustrate my point:

$$(1.00)^{365} = 1.00$$

$$(1.01)^{365} = 37.7$$

[iii]

Now here we have simple mathematics at its best! Please excuse the accountant deep within me. In the first example, we see that if you consistently do the same thing every day for 365 days of the year, at the end of the year you will be at the exact same place as you were at the beginning of the year. Whereas if you were to put in an extra 0.01% effort and work every day for 365 days then at the end of the year you will end up at a level 37.7% higher than where you were at the beginning of the year.

To bring the principle back home, I will apply this to going to the gym and achieving your dream body. Let's say you have made that infamous *New Year's Resolution* (yes, infamous because New Year's Resolutions don't usually have a very high success rate) and you decide that as from 1 January you will start working on losing weight, eating healthy, and exercising regularly for you to achieve your dream body. If from 1 January this resolution just remains in your head and you neglect to take any active steps towards getting your dream body, by the time 31 December of that year arrives, you would find that you still have the same body that you had on 1 January - 365 days earlier! You had a full 365 days to work towards your dream body and put a dent in the scale but because you did absolutely nothing, you have no results to show a full calendar year later.

The opposite is the powerful "secret" I wish to share with you and I pray you grasp it. The power in transformation lies in putting in small, consistent effort each and every single day! Of course, the greater the effort daily, the greater the results at the end of 365 days. But for now, let's say you put in 0.01% effort every day for 365 days. Meaning you either eat healthy for the entire day or put in a 30-minute workout a day. If you consistently do this for 365 days you will see that after 365 days you would have lost more than 5kgs and your body would be visibly more toned. As I said earlier though, the more effort you put into the two actions the greater the results at the end of the calendar year. It all depends on YOU though. What I definitely guarantee you is if you put in the consistent effort then you WILL get results that you will love.

Now I know in theory this is a GREAT thought - being consistent. Every single day. Without fail. But knowing how humans are and how inconsistent we are, this seems like an almost impossible task. I would like you to know that it IS possible and the reason you are reading this book is to learn how to be consistent. Here are my techniques to assist you in being consistent in your daily efforts so that at the end of 365 days, you would have achieved your goal no matter what it may be.

1.   Remember Your WHY?

Instant gratification is, in my opinion, the main reason for the demise of our current generation when it comes to sticking to a prolonged process and achieving their goals. As humans, we focus on the now and we expect to see results immediately after putting in minimal short-term effort. Many of us were not raised with the mental training to forget about seeing the short-term results, trusting the process, and continuing to work towards a goal straight through to the end. Even if after three months you are not seeing the desired results. Just believing and trusting the process and path you are on <u>will</u> yield the end goal that you so deeply desire but only IF you put in the consistent work!

During the process, most people end up quitting because they allow the discouragement brought on from not seeing any results crush their spirits and momentum which then subsequently leads them to give up. Whenever you feel this way, a simple technique to refuel your momentum and boost your energy is to remember your why. Remind yourself of why you started this journey in the first place. The reason you are feeling disheartened is that you have lost sight of what it is that you are trying to achieve and how that end goal will make you feel. Remember in Chapter 3 **(Emotions Fuel your Actions)** I spoke about how your emotions give energy to a thought to bring it to fruition. So to reignite that spark within you, you have to sit down and envision your end goal and attach a positive emotion to it until you clearly see yourself achieving that goal in your mind and you can vividly feel the strong positive emotions of having achieved it. Try it now. Do you feel the strong emotions? Now let those strong feelings flow through your whole body and let it revive your lethargic body and give it that boost it needs to keep going.

A mother working two jobs while studying part-time finds consistency in her actions to show up at both jobs every day and still study at night because daily she reminds herself of her why: to earn money to take care of her child and to obtain a degree that will get her a better paying job so that her son can live a better life than she did when she was growing up.

2.   Incongruence Within Your Subconscious

I am sure you have heard of the popular saying: "One part within me wants to do X but then the other part of me wants to do Y". Literally speaking, this is saying that two separate parts within us want to do opposing things, yet we are one whole person! How is this possible? The reason behind this is because there is a conflict between what we consciously believe and what we subconsciously believe to be true. An example of this would be if you want to lose weight consciously but yet at the same time you subconsciously still believe that you are not worthy of a sexy body and that you are still fat! This incongruence (conflict) within you is what hinders you from being consistent because deep down inside (on a subconscious level) you do not TRULY believe in what you are trying to achieve on the outside (conscious). In order to achieve consistency, you need to ensure that both your subconscious and conscious are in agreement with each other so that they are in harmony and are on the same path to achieving your goal, which ensures daily consistent action towards achieving it.

3.   Make The Desired Behaviour A Habit

Adding on to the previous point of making sure your conscious and subconscious are in agreement, the way to get your subconscious on board is to re-programme it to believe what you are trying to achieve, even if it is not true at the present moment. Reprogramming of the subconscious in any case is always going to be about re-programming it to something that is not true <u>as yet</u>. It takes 21 days to make a behaviour a habit. So for instance, if you want to create the habit of drinking 8 glasses of water a day, do this consistently by force for 21 days and you will see that by day 30 your body will automatically crave 8 glasses of water without you actively putting in the conscious effort to drink them.

CONCLUSION

If you are reading this then well done! It means you have completed reading my book on life transformation. My hope is that you found all this information very useful and after all this reading you have this key takeaway: the life you desire is within your reach; you just have to do the work.

You have learnt a lot of theories through this book and if you require coaching with implementing them practically, which will then bring about the change you need, then please feel free to contact me for one-on-one coaching. I will be able to help you break through what has been holding you back from living the life you desire. If you present this book to me when you start my one-on-one coaching then you will receive a 25% discount on my full coaching course.

You can read up more on my coaching services on my website: www.elevatetransformationcoaching.com

The areas I specialize in assisting my clients with are:

- Life Transformation Coaching
- Discovering your potential
- Low self-esteem
- Anxiety elimination
- Depression

- Trauma
- Weight-loss
- Public speaking
- Career advancement
- Entrepreneurship coaching

ABOUT THE AUTHOR

Tafadzwa Makombe is a qualified Chartered Accountant by profession, Certified Life Coach, Certified Neuro-Linguistic Programming Practitioner, Entrepreneur, and Humanitarian.

Tafadzwa studied accounting at the University of Cape Town and completed her Chartered Accounting articles through Deloitte and Touche. After passing two Board Exams and qualifying as a Chartered Accountant in 2015, she went on to work at Anglo American for two years where the whole department she worked for got retrenched. This was a pivotal moment for Tafadzwa because all her life she was told to work hard, go to university, get a degree, and get a good-paying job, which she did. But then, at a young age in a supposedly stable career, she was retrenched at the end of December 2017 and everything she grew up believing was disproved. It's at this point that she learnt that you can fail at what you don't want, so you might as well go after what you love! This is when she began exploring entrepreneurship and in 2019, she started her own coaching business which focuses on transformational life coaching, public speaking, career coaching, self-esteem building, and anxiety alleviation.

Since the inception of her coaching business, Tafadzwa has helped hundreds of people to unlock their potential through overcoming self-doubt, anxiety, and self-sabotage. She has helped them to set up their goals and achieve their dreams through the transformation of their mindsets: how they view the world and what they believe is possible.

Tafadzwa is brilliant. She is bright. She is a radiant being of light. She is an outstanding peak performer. She is a dynamic life transformer. Tafadzwa has an amazing natural gift of being able to connect with her audience and get to the root of their limiting beliefs which hold them back from living their best possible life whether it is mentally, spiritually, physically, financially, career-wise or even rela-tionally. Tafadzwa's diligent work ethic and deep-rooted care to see people and teams within corporations become the best versions of themselves in order to achieve out-standing and tangible results are the reasons why she is one of the top speakers to invite to come to transform a group of people.

BIBLIOGRAPHY

i   Mind Power image (page 17), https://www.linkedin.com/pulse/mind-power-thoughts-sreejith-nair

ii   Self-doubt image (page 99), http://theawkwardyeti.com/comic/burden/

iii Consistent effort image (page 108), https://www.pinterest.com/pin/456693837090054213/

www.ingramcontent.com/pod-product-compliance
Lightning Source LLC
Chambersburg PA
CBHW022106050726
47591CB00002B/697